Children's Torah

Activity Book 5
By Belinda McCallion

This book Belongs to:

_____

How to use this book:

These worksheets have been especially designed for easy photocopy duplication.

Each lesson has 3 parts; a Torah, a Haftara and a B'rit Hadashah.

The main page of each part is the instruction page. This is not intended to replace the actual reading of the portion but to be a tool that can be used to summarise the readings and find a few key messages from the readings.

The activity page relates to the lesson and is intended to be used to reinforce the messages. This page caters to a wide age group, as there is always a picture to colour and a more difficult activity. Each activity sheet ranges in difficulty level dependant on the lesson. There is an answer page at the back of the book if you get stuck.

Table of Contents

Parasha 44

דברים פרשת D'varim (Words) Deuteronomy 1:1-3:22

Memory Verse

"Likewise in the desert, where you saw how *ADONAI* your God carried you, like a man carries his child, along the entire way you travelled until you arrived at this place.."

Deut 1:31 CJB

Did You Know?

The fight for this land still goes on today.

STORY SUMMARY

Exodus Summary: The children of Isra'el are about to enter the Promised Land. They have been on their journey for forty years. Moshe (Moses) gives them an overview of their journey so far. He talks about the places they went and the events along the way. He tells how ADONAI has led them like children, yet they were untrusting of ADONAI's leadership. He also reminds them about the lands they were called to conquer or leave in peace and why.

WORD FOCUS

Refa'im: 'Giants.' The cities Isra'el were called to destroy were cities of giants. The cities of Isra'el's relatives, such as Esav (Esau) and Lot, they were to leave alone.

MAIN MESSAGE

Everything is brought to a head and given some perspective in this summary. It is the end of one chapter and the beginning of a new one. Moshe has learnt some things on his journey, and he is hopeful that the rest of Isra'el has too, and encourages them to remember these lessons when they enter the land. We always need to remember where we have come from to appreciate where we are going. We cannot always see ADONAI's hand in our life until we have come through a situation and look back.

LOOK BACK   LOOK FORWARD   REMEMBER

Promise

Deut 1:38 CJB

"Y'hoshua the son of Nun, your assistant — he will go in there. So encourage him, because he will enable Isra'el to take possession of it."

Note: Parental discretion advised when reading biblical narrative.

D'varim Deuteronomy 1:1-3:22 Activity Sheet

King Og's Bed

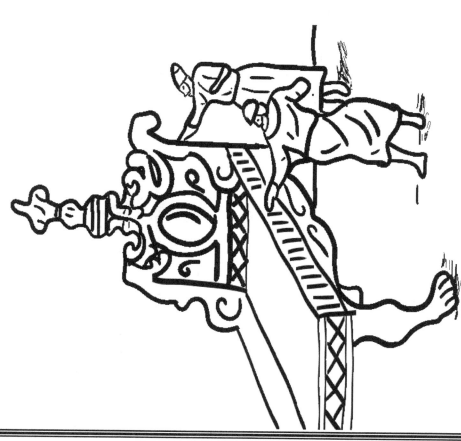

"Og, king of Bashan was the last survivor of the Refa'im. His bed was made of iron; it is still in Rabbah with the people of Amon. It was nine cubits long and four cubits wide, using the normal cubit [thirteen-and-a-half by six feet]." Deut 3:11 CJB

Giant Troubles

Some times our problems look giant. ADONAI can help you with your giant problems.

Avoid the giants to make your way through the grid safely. You may go diagonally, up, down or across.

OUT

IN

3

Haftara of Affliction 3.

Isaiah 1:1-27

Promise

Isaiah 1:26 CJB

"I will restore your judges as at first and your advisers as at the beginning. After that, you will be called the City of Righteousness, Faithful City."

Haftara 44 (Prophets)

Memory Verse

"But I will also turn my hand against you! I will cleanse your impurities as with lye and remove all your alloyed base metal."

Isaiah 1:25 CJB

Did You Know?

ADONAI does not wait for us to be sorry, He *causes* us to be sorry. Even this we cannot do in our own strength.

STORY SUMMARY

ADONAI Warns Isra'el: ADONAI, through Yesha'yahu (Isaiah), tells again how His children have turned their back on Him. If it were not for the few faithful people, they would have been destroyed like Sodom. We are then given a glimpse of what life will be like if Isra'el changes its ways, and begins to obey ADONAI. Not only with their outward actions, such as sacrifices and feast-keeping, but from their hearts.

WORD FOCUS

Bedil: 'Tin.' Meaning 'that which is separated from precious metal.' ADONAI describes His people as metal being purified by this process.

MAIN MESSAGE

This is the third and final lesson focusing on the mistakes of ADONAI's people. Again Isra'el has disappointed ADONAI. It is interesting that ADONAI's solution to their rebellion is not to cut them off, but to purify them. ADONAI gives us every opportunity to belong to His righteous kingdom. Even after all the evil we do, it is ADONAI who causes us to repent so He can accept us.

REPENT   **RIGHTOUSNESS**   **REFINE**

Pathway to Happiness

Life is full of decisions. Choosing to do the right thing leads us on a path to happiness and blessings. At each fork in the road, one way will lead on to the path of happiness, and the other will either lead back to the place of unhappiness or lead nowhere. Can you find the path that leads to happiness?

Do Good

"Learn to do good! Seek justice, relieve the oppressed, defend orphans, plead for the widow." Isaiah 1:17 CJB

John
14:1-3

B'rit Hadashah 44
(Newer Testament)

MAIN MESSAGE

The apostles, just as the children of Isra'el, were worried about what was ahead for them. Yeshua, like Moshe, gives final words of encouragement to see them through these tough times ahead. We continue to hold on to these last words of hope, and look forward to the time when Yeshua will come back as our reigning king, Maschiach Ben David.

PROMISE

"In my Father's house are many places to live. If there weren't, I would have told you; because I am going there to prepare a place for you. Since I am going and preparing a place for you, I will return to take you with me; so that where I am, you may be also." John 14:2-3 CJB

DID YOU KNOW?

Revelation tells us more about this special place Yeshua is preparing.

STORY SUMMARY

Yeshua's Last Words: Yeshua encourages His disciples to carry on, with some words of hope. He tells them to keep believing, and to look forward to the time when He will come back and give them a special place to live.

WORD FOCUS – TRUST

Chasah: Trust— to lean on
Betach: Trust— to cling to
Yachal: Trust— the hope of knowing
Aman: Trust— to be firm

Trust is not an abstract thought, but defined actions.

MEMORY VERSE

"Don't let yourselves be disturbed. Trust in G–d and trust in me." John 14:1 CJB

John 14:1-3 Activity Sheet

New Jerusalem

"Also I saw the holy city, New Yerushalayim, coming down out of heaven from G-d, prepared like a bride beautifully dressed for her husband." Revelation 21:2 CJB

Trust

Trust is an action. Choose the action for each situation that requires trust. Circle the right answer.

1. Your mum can't find the door key. Do you:

A. Ask ADONAI to help you find a way in and lean on Him?

B. Smash the window and get in.

2. Your friend tells you G-d is not real. Do you:

A. Believe him because he is your friend and you know he is smart.

B. Choose to keep believing in the hope that you know?

3. You have just lost someone you love. Do you:

A. Take some drugs to help you forget your pain?

B. Cling to ADONAI through prayer and reading your bible?

4. A leader says, if you believe in G-d you will be punished. Do you:

A. Keep your faith in G-d no matter what happens?

B. Deny your faith?

Parasha 45

Memory Verse

"In order to obey the *mitzvot* of *ADONAI* your God which I am giving you, do not add to what I am saying, and do not subtract from it."

Deut 4:2 CJB

Did You Know?

It is possible that the law, as written on the first tablets of stone, was not identical to the second.

שוָאֶתְחַנַּן **Vaetchanan** (I pleaded) Deuteronomy 3:23-7:11

STORY SUMMARY

Moshe calls Isra'el to remember ADONAI: Moshe (Moses) continues his final speech to Isra'el. He makes sure Isra'el knows it is because of their rebellion that he is not allowed to enter the Promised Land. Moshe then pleas with Isra'el to remember the Law as they go into the Promised Land, so their lives will go well.

WORD FOCUS

Sh'ma, Yisra'el! ADONAI Eloheinu, ADONAI echad: Hear, Isra'el! ADONAI our God, ADONAI is one. This is the Shema. It is a very popular verse. Deut 6:4.

MAIN MESSAGE

Moshe says, when the other nations see Isra'el following ADONAI's laws, they will think Isra'el is wise. ADONAI's laws are better than any laws other nations can come up with. They are based on faith and justice. Out of all the laws around today, ADONAI's laws are still the best and they have stood the test of time. If we follow them, we will be blessed, and the nations around us will be blessed also.

REMEMBER   **OBEY**   **HAVE FAITH**

Promise
Deut 4:1 CJB

"Now, Isra'el, listen to the laws and rulings I am teaching you, in order to follow them, so that you will live; then you will go in and take possession of the land that *ADONAI*, the God of your fathers, is giving you."

Vaetchanan Deut 3:23-7:11 Activity Sheet

Laws

If you were the leader of a country, what would your 10 most important laws be? Think about each law, Is it better for you as the leader, or for the people?

1	
2	
3	
4	
5	
6	
7	
8	
9	
10	

Moshe Sees the Land

"Climb up to the top of Pisgah and look out to the west, north, south and east. Look with your eyes — but you will not go across this Yarden." Deut 3:27 CJB

Shabbat Nahamu

Isaiah 40:1-26

Haftara 45 (Prophets)

Memory Verse

"Here comes *ADONAI ELO-HIM* with power, and His arm will rule for Him. Look! His reward is with Him, and His recompense is before Him."
Isaiah 40:10 CJB

Did You Know?

ADONAI loves you, even when you are naughty.

Promise

Isaiah 40:1-2 CJB

"'Comfort and keep comforting my people,' says your God. 'Tell Yerushalayim to take heart; proclaim to her that she has completed her time of service, that her guilt has been paid off, that she has received at the hand of *ADONAI* double for all her sins.'"

STORY SUMMARY

ADONAI Sends Hope: ADONAI, through Yeshayahu (Isaiah), gives a message of great hope for Isra'el. The time has come when they are to return from exile. Although they have not earned this right through good behaviour, ADONAI says they have paid a big enough price, and ADONAI is coming back for His children with great glory and splendour.

WORD FOCUS

Nahamu: 'Comfort.' We get the name of this Shabbat because it follows the 9th of Aviv. The three weeks of mourning over the destruction of the Temples has ended. Shabbat Hahamu celebrates reconciliation, when ADONAI shows His great mercy.

MAIN MESSAGE

This message applied to Isra'el in Yeshayahu's day, and it applies to the final generation on the earth. The exiles that are scattered all over the world will be gathered again by ADONAI. This is not because they deserve it, but because He is faithful to keep His promises. As believers we hope to be the final generation and be counted in the great gathering.

REPENT   HOPE   COMFORT

Shabbat Nahamu Isaiah 40:1-26 Activity Sheet

Stars in the Sky

ADONAI put the stars in the sky, and He knows them by name.

According to these verses below, who else did ADONAI call by name and compare to stars?

"But now this is what ADONAI says, He who created you, Ya'akov, He who formed you, Isra'el: 'Don't be afraid, for I have redeemed you; I am calling you by your name; you are mine.'"

Isaiah 43:1 CJB

"I will make your descendants as numerous as the stars in the sky, I will give all these lands to your descendants, and by your descendants all the nations of the earth will bless themselves."

Genesis 26:4 CJB

_____

Stars

"Turn your eyes to the heavens! See who created these?
He brings out the army of them in sequence, summoning each by name. Through His great might and His massive strength."

Isaiah 40:26 CJB

Luke
18:1-7

B'rit Hadashah 45
(Newer Testament)

STORY SUMMARY

Persistent Prayer: Yeshua tells the story of a woman who asks over and over again for the same thing until, in order for her to leave him alone, the judge grants her request. Yeshua says we should pray like this.

WORD FOCUS

Kavanat ha lev: Is the true essence of prayer, which means to be in a state of worship, concentration and single-mindedness. Unless we pray in this way we will not fully connect to ADONAI. We need to pray with our hearts.

MEMORY VERSE

"...They must always keep praying and not lose heart."
Luke 18:1 CJB

Main Message

Moshe is persistent when he asks ADONAI about seeing the Promised Land. Although his request was not granted, this shows, persistent prayer is good. When we see things becoming sinful around us, our best defence is prayer, and a lot of it.

PROMISE

"Now won't G-d grant justice to His chosen people who cry out to Him day and night? Is He delaying long over them?"
Luke 18:7 CJB

DID YOU KNOW?

Prayer means to talk with ADONAI. When Adam and Eve talked to ADONAI in the garden, this was prayer.

Luke 18:1-7 Activity Sheet

Prayer

There are many different ways to pray. Chronicles 20:6 –12 is a great example of the 5 P's Prayer. Practice using these in your prayer.

1. Praise

Praise ADONAI for His good qualities; especially those which relate to your problem.

2. Past

Think about when ADONAI has helped you in the past, and thank Him for this.

3. Promise

Claim a bible promise about your situation.

4. Problem

Tell ADONAI what is on your mind.

5. Praise

Thank Him before you see any answers.

Example: "Blessed are You ADONAI creator of the Universe, who heals our bodies. Thank-you for making me well when I had the flu last month. Your word says 'I called to you for help and you healed me.' Loving father I call to You now and ask You please to heal my leg. Thank-you that You hear our prayers, and for Your healing touch. Amen."

Prayer

"There was also in that town a widow who kept coming to him saying, 'Give me a judgement against the man who is trying to ruin me.'" Luke 18:3 CJB

Parasha 46

פרשת עקב Eikev (Because) Deuteronomy 7:12-11:25

Memory Verse

"Therefore, you are to store up these words of Mine in your heart and in all your being; tie them on your hand as a sign; put them at the front of a headband around your forehead."

Deut 11:18 CJB

Did You Know?

Deuteronomy is the last book of Moshe before he died.

STORY SUMMARY

ADONAI's Promise and Conditions: Moshe (Moses) tells Isra'el; If they continue to obey ADONAI, they will live in safety. He reminds them of the benefits of keeping ADONAI's laws, including conquering opposing nations. However, this is not because Isra'el is a righteous people, but because the nations are very wicked. After reminding Isra'el where they went wrong in the past, Moshe leaves them with the promise of a plentiful land flowing with milk and honey, if they are faithful.

WORD FOCUS

He-Sed: 'Kindness' or 'Mercy.' ADONAI's covenant was a covenant of hesed.

MAIN MESSAGE

There was a battle for survival going on. Although ADONAI is a G-d of mercy, in this case, mercy towards the enemy would lead to Isra'el's destruction. ADONAI does not want us to be half-hearted in dealing with sin in our lives. He wants us to stand boldly against it. We are also warned against bringing evil things into our homes. Troubled times help to show our true heart and polish our character. When we have life too easy, we can forget our need for ADONAI, and be tempted to think that we created our own good fortune.

REMEMBER   OBEY   STAND STRONG

Promise

Deut. 7:12 CJB

"Because you are listening to these rulings, keeping and obeying them, *ADONAI* your G-d will keep with you the covenant and mercy that He swore to your ancestors."

Note: Parental discretion advised when reading biblical narrative.

14

Eikev Deut 7:12-11:25 Activity Sheet

A Land of milk and Honey

"And so that you will live long in the land ADONAI swore to give to your ancestors and their descendants, a land flowing with milk and honey." Deut 11:9 CJB

Detestable Things

Deuteronomy 7:26 says, not to bring any detestable thing into your house, in case you share in the curse that is on it. Have you ever thought that objects could carry curses? What are some things you think ADONAI might find detestable for you to bring into your house?

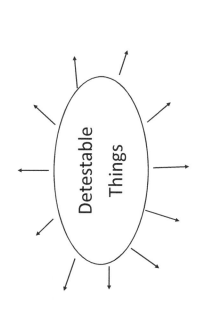

Detestable Things

Yeshayahu

Isaiah 49:14-51:3

Haftara 46 (Prophets)

Memory Verse

"I have engraved you on the palms of My hands, your walls are always before Me."
Isaiah 49:16 CJB

Did You Know?

ADONAI is still waiting for His people to come back to Him fully.

STORY SUMMARY

Isra'el Feels Abandoned: This Haftara continues the theme of comfort. Isra'el is in exile and they are feeling the results of their sin. They fear that ADONAI has rejected them forever; all their hope is gone. Through Yeshayahu (Isaiah), ADONAI responds in love and kindness telling Isra'el that He could never forget them, they are constantly on His mind. He has engraved them into the palms of His hands. ADONAI brings hope back by telling Isra'el of a day when He will make all things right.

WORD FOCUS

Kaph: 'Flat or hollow of the palm of the hand.' This is where ADONAI said Isra'el is inscribed. Could this have anything to do with the nails in Yeshua's hands?

MAIN MESSAGE

This message tells us, there is always hope. No matter how hard things get, or how far we have gone away from ADONAI, He is always willing to welcome us back. He never left us. Today we are sill living with that hope of a brighter future, where ADONAI is in full control.

REPENT   HOPE   COMFORT

Promise

Isaiah 51:3 CJB

"For ADONAI will comfort Tziyon, will comfort all her ruined places, will make her desert like 'Eden, her Aravah like the garden of ADONAI. Joy and gladness will be there, thanksgiving and the sound of music."

Yeshayahu Isaiah 49:14-51:3 Activity Sheet

ADONAI's Promise

When Isra'el was worrying about being destroyed forever, ADONAI made a great promise about their future descendants. Use the word endings shapes to complete the verse from Isaiah 49:18 CJB.

You can use the endings more than once.

"As sure__ as I am

ali__, y__ wi__ we__

th__ a__ li Jewe__,

ado__ yourse__ wi__

th__ li__ a bri__."

Return

"I am beckoning to the nations, raising my banner for the peoples. They will bring your sons in their arms and carry your daughters on their shoulders."

Isaiah 49:22 CJB

17

1 Corinthians   B'rit Hadashah 46
13   (Newer Testament)

STORY SUMMARY

What is Love? Paul describes love as being patient and kind. It is not jealous, boastful, arrogant, proud, rude, selfish, angry, or resentful. Love doesn't rejoice in evil but rejoices in truth. It bears, believes, hopes and endures all things. Love never ends.

WORD FOCUS

Arek: 'Long.' As in, patient or slow to anger. This is the first attribute of love listed. It is very hard to show love when we get angry.

MEMORY VERSE

"But for now, three things last — trust, hope, love; and the greatest of these is love."
1 Corinthians 13:13 CJB

MAIN MESSAGE

Although we see ADONAI calling for the complete destruction of the wicked nations, we also see in Deuteronomy 10:19 a commission to love the foreigners. Therefore, ADONAI was not saying that everyone who was not Isra'el was wicked. He did not want Isra'el to be prideful. He wanted them to love others. Paul again affirms this need to love others in Corinthians.

PROMISE

"For now we see obscurely in a mirror, but then it will be face to face. Now I know partly; then I will know fully, just as G-d has fully known me." 1 Cor 13:12 CJB

DID YOU KNOW?

Love is a fruit of the Spirit. Without the Ruach, we are not able to show true love.

1 Corinthians 13 Activity Sheet

Love is Kind

"Love is patient and kind, not jealous, not boastful, not proud, rude or selfish, not easily angered, and it keeps no record of wrongs." 1 Cor 13: 4-5

Love

1 Corinthian 13:4-5 lists six things love is not. What would the loving response be? Write the opposite to these words in the spaces provided.

Jealous/ Envious: _____

Boastful: _____

Proud: _____

Rude: _____

Selfish: _____

Easily Angered: _____

ראה Re'eh (See) Deuteronomy 11:26-16:17

Parasha 47

Memory Verse

"And you are to take care to follow all the laws and rulings I am setting before you today."

Deut 11:32 CJB

Did You Know?

Mt Ebal is said to be in modern-day Samaria.

STORY SUMMARY

ADONAI's Laws Continue: Moshe (Moses) continues to tells Isra'el how ADONAI expects them to live while in the land, and the importance of serving ADONAI only. One mountain is set apart for blessings, and another for curses. If they follow ADONAI, they will be blessed. Moshe then reminds them of the consequences of worshipping other gods. This is followed by the retelling of ADONAI's laws for food, tithe, the seventh year, the sacrifices and offerings, and the festivals. He also tells them that many of these things needed to be practiced only in the place ADONAI would tell them.

WORD FOCUS

Ebal: 'Rocky.' This is the name of the cursed mountain. Life will be rocky without the blessings of ADONAI.

MAIN MESSAGE

ADONAI knew how easy it would be for Isra'el to be tempted to follow other gods. Without the boundaries of His law, we fall into temptation and sin. We need to take ADONAI's ways seriously, and sometimes not mix His ways with the ways of the world. We don't always understand His ways and sometimes even question them. However, every time we ignore ADONAI's ways, and follow our own ways, we end up in trouble.

REMEMBER   OBEY   STAND STRONG

Promise

Deut 11:26 CJB

"See, I am setting before you today a blessing and a curse —the blessing, if you listen to the *mitzvot* of ADONAI your G-d that I am giving you today."

Note: Parental discretion advised when reading biblical narrative.

Re'eh Deut 11:26-16:17 Activity Sheet

Blessings and Curses

"When ADONAI your God brings you into the land you are entering in order to take possession of it, you are to put the blessing on Mount G'rizim and the curse on Mount Eival." Deut 11:9 CJB

Blessings of the Land

ADONAI told Isra'el that they would have plenty to eat in the land. Remember to thank ADONAI for the gift of food.

What foods would you like to thank ADONAI for? Draw or write them here.

Yeshayahu

Isaiah 54:11–55:5

Promise

Isaiah 54:13 CJB

"All your children will be taught by *ADONAI*; your children will have great peace."

STORY SUMMARY

A Vision of Tziyon (Zion): Yeshayahu (Isaiah) prophesies of a time when Tziyon will be restored. It will be more brilliant than ever before. ADONAI will the be the ruler; people will be blessed and live in peace.

WORD FOCUS

Yayin: 'Wine.' **Chalab:** 'Milk.' In Jewish tradition the wine and milk are said to represent spiritual sustenance.

MAIN MESSAGE

The restoration of creation is ADONAI's desire and our deepest longing. ADONAI is working out His plan to restore what was lost when Adam and Chavah (Eve) sinned. We all need to be restored. This can start in us today if we repent of our sins and ask ADONAI to be the king of our life.

REPENT　　　　**HOPE**　　　　**COMFORT**

Haftara 47 (Prophets)

Memory Verse

"All you who are thirsty, come to the water! You without money, come, buy, and eat! Yes, come! Buy wine and milk without money — it's free!"

Isaiah 55:1 CJB

Did You Know?

Revelation talks about a new Yerushalayim (Jerusalem) that comes down out of Heaven from ADONAI.

Yeshayahu Isaiah 54:11-55:5 Activity Sheet

Brilliant City

Follow the colour key, and the description in the verses below, to colour this picture.

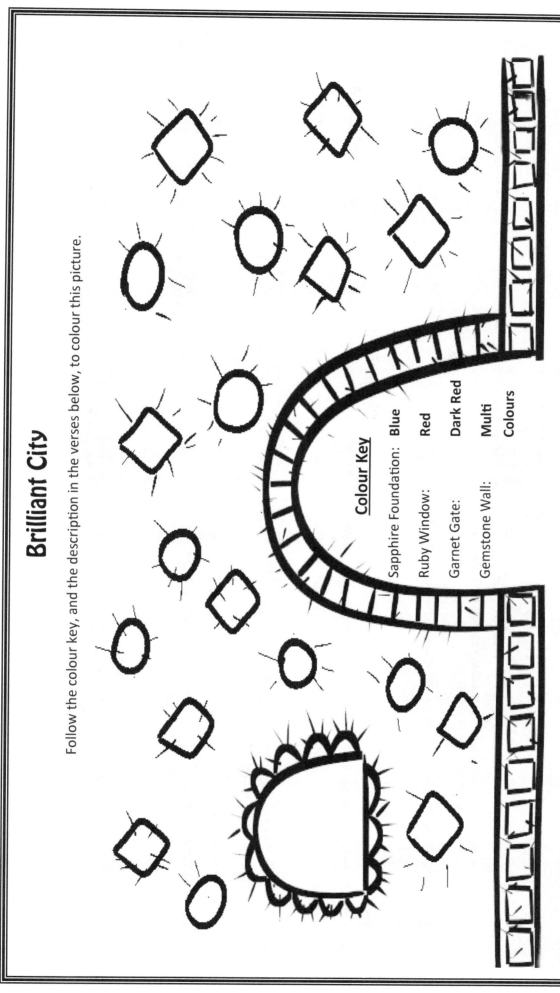

Colour Key

Sapphire Foundation:	**Blue**
Ruby Window:	**Red**
Garnet Gate:	**Dark Red**
Gemstone Wall:	**Multi Colours**

"Storm-ravaged [city], unconsoled, I will set your stones in the finest way, lay your foundations with sapphires, make your windows shine with rubies, your gates with garnet, your walls with gemstones." Isaiah 54:11-12 CJB

Romans 7:7-18

B'rit Hadashah 47
(Newer Testament)

STORY SUMMARY

Defending the Torah: Paul outlines that without the Torah there is no definition of sin, nor anything to prompt us to change. He affirms that the Torah is not the problem, but the sinful state of mankind.

WORD FOCUS

Torah: The law of ADONAI as revealed to Moshe (Moses) in the first five books of the bible.

MEMORY VERSE

"Everything I am commanding you, you are to take care to do. Do not add to it or subtract from it."
Deuteronomy 13:1 CJB*

MAIN MESSAGE

Some people say that Yeshua and Paul taught against the Torah. This passage shows that Paul didn't teach against the Torah. Yeshua also said that the Torah would not change. The parasha this week warns against adding to or taking away from the law. There are some things that did change when Yeshua came, but not His law. Paul says the law is how we know what sin is, and makes us see our need for a saviour.

PROMISE

"What a miserable creature I am! Who will rescue me from this body bound for death? Thanks be to G-d[, He will]! – through Yeshua the Messiah, our Lord!" Romans 7:24-25 CJB

DID YOU KNOW?

Paul knew the Torah very well, and he followed its principles.

*12:32 in other translations

Romans 7:7-18 Activity Sheet

Adding to and Taking Away From

The Bible says we are not to add to ADONAI's law or take away from it. Matthew 5:18 below has letters added to or taken away from the words. There is one change in each word. Rewrite it as it should be.

Yesh inded! Ic telle your tat funtil haven sand eart plass way, note sho munch s al gyud for va stoke swill passt fom th Torahs — noot untill evrything thath mut hapen hasp appened.

_____

_____

_____

_____

Knowledge of Sin

"Therefore, what are we to say? That the Torah is sinful? Heaven forbid! Rather, the function of the Torah was that without it, I would not have known what sin is. For example, I would not have become conscious of what greed is if the Torah had not said, **'Thou shalt not covet.'"** Hebrews 7:7 CJB

Parasha 48

שופטים Shof'tim
(Judges) Deuteronomy 16:18-21:9

Memory Verse

"Justice, only justice, you must pursue; so that you will live and inherit the land ADONAI your God is giving you."
Deut 16:20 CJB

Did You Know?

Deuteronomy 17:17 warns kings against having many wives and riches. These were the very things that caused David and Solomon to stumble.

STORY SUMMARY

Three Kinds of Leadership: Moshe (Moses), in his final address to Isra'el before entering the land, discusses civil laws and how to run the nation. Firstly, advice is given to the judges, then to kings, priests and prophets. If Isra'el follows the ways set out, they will prosper in the land, but the ways of other god's are forbidden.

WORD FOCUS

Mishpat: 'Judgement.' It also includes governing, which is the legal authority to set up and interpret laws, declare verdicts and carry out sentences. ADONAI is the most righteous judge.

MAIN MESSAGE

How nations are run has a direct impact on how blessed they will be, or how they will prosper. Many laws today are based on principles found in the Bible. Places that have done this have experienced the most prosperity. When leaders turn against ADONAI, the whole nation suffers. We should pray for our leaders. They have an important job to do.

GOVERNMENT   JUSTICE   JUDGEMENT

Promise
Deut 18:15 CJB

"*ADONAI* will raise up for you a prophet like me from among yourselves, from your own kinsmen. You are to pay attention to him."

Note: Parental discretion advised when reading biblical narrative

Shof'tim Deuteronomy 16:18-21:9 Activity Sheet

The Occult

We are warned against occult practices in Deuteronomy 18:10-11.
These days we see so much of these things, especially on television.
Match the titles with the definitions. Some are very similar.

Enchanter	A person who uses special powers and ceremonies to predict future events
Necromancer	A person who sees future events through dreams or visions
Soothsayer	A person who uses magic or spells
Diviner	A person who has/claims to have magical powers.
Sorcerer/Wizard	A person who uses magic to talk to the dead

City of Refuge

"Divide the territory of your land, which *ADONAI* your G-d is having you inherit, into three parts; and prepare the roads, so that any killer can flee to these cities." Deuteronomy 19:3 CJB

Yeshayahu

Isaiah 51:12-52:12

Memory Verse

"How beautiful on the mountains are the feet of him who brings good news, proclaiming *shalom*, bringing good news of good things, announcing salvation and saying to Tziyon, 'Your God is King!'"

Isaiah 52:7 CJB

Did You Know?

Tradition says that Isra'el fell unconscious at Sinai when they met with ADONAI, and needed to be revived by Him.

Promise

Isaiah 51:16 CJB

"I have put My words in your mouth and covered you with the shadow of My hand, in order to plant the skies [anew], lay the foundations of the earth [anew] and say to Tziyon, 'You are My people.'"

STORY SUMMARY

ADONAI Tells of the Final Redemption: ADONAI, through Yesha'yahu (Isaiah), comforts Isra'el and calms their fears. They worry about returning to the land, only to face more persecution. ADONAI is comforting them by telling them, in the end, He will personally draw them and be their king. They will see Him face to face or 'eye to eye' and they will live in peace forever.

WORD FOCUS

Mashiach: 'Anointed one.' The Mashiach will be anointed as king.

MAIN MESSAGE

This is what is referred to as the age of mashiach. This prophecy was a wonder to Isra'el. They did not think it possible to see ADONAI face to face. The parasha reminds us that Isra'el asked not to see ADONAI's face again in case they die. "Who can see ADONAI and live?" they asked. This passage shows that in this age of mashiach they will see Him and live.

HOPE   COMFORT   WONDER

Yeshayahu Isaiah 51:12-52:12 Activity Sheet

Our Redemption

Unscramble Isaiah 52:10 to reveal what all the ends of the earth will see. Number the boxes in their correct order.

☐ and all the ends of the earth will see

☐ in the sight of every nation

☐ the salvation of our G-d

☐ ADONAI Has bared His holy arm

Foundations of the earth

"You have forgotten *ADONAI*, your maker, who stretched out the heavens and laid the foundations of the earth." Isaiah 51:13 CJB

James
2:1-11

B'rit Hadashah 48
(Newer Testament)

STORY SUMMARY

Righteous Judgement: James gives council to the Messianic congregation. They are not to show favouritism to the rich and oppress the poor. In this way they will be following the Torah principle of loving their neighbour.

WORD FOCUS

Anav: 'Poor,' also meaning 'afflicted, humble and meek.' To be poor is often expressed as a character trait, or a condition ADONAI values.

MEMORY VERSE

"My brothers, practice the faith of our Lord Yeshua, the glorious Messiah, without showing favoritism." James 2:1 CJB

MAIN MESSAGE

This follows the parasha theme of justice in leadership. ADONAI is consistent with His desire for justice among His people. Regardless of their social status, everyone is important to ADONAI. He wants us to treat everyone with respect, not only rich or famous people.

PROMISE

"Listen, my dear brothers, hasn't G-d chosen the poor of the world to be rich in faith and to receive the Kingdom which He promised to those who love Him?" James 2:5CJB

DID YOU KNOW?

Having hard times in our lives helps us to be rich in faith. Being rich in faith is better than being rich with money.

James 2:1-11 Activity Sheet

Favoritism

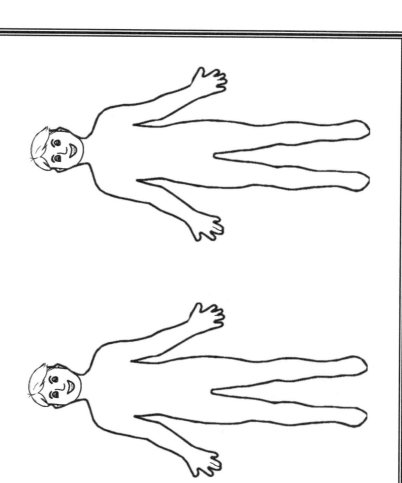

"But if you show favouritism, your actions constitute sin, since you are convicted under the *Torah* as transgressors." James 2:9 CJB

Equality

The clothes we wear or the colour of our skin is not what makes us important. We are important because we are ADONAI's own creation. These two figures are the same now. Draw expensive clothes on one, and worn out clothes on the other. Does this really make one more important than the other?

Parasha 49

כי־תצא Ki Teitzei (When you go out) Deuteronomy 21:10-25:19

Memory Verse

"Rather, remember that you were a slave in Egypt; and ADONAI your G-d redeemed you from there. That is why I am ordering you to do this."

Deut 24:18 CJB

Did You Know?

It is said, that seventy-two of the 613 instructions are given in this Torah portion.

STORY SUMMARY

Brotherly Love: ADONAI, through Moshe (Moses), instructs Isra'el about relationships with foreigners and amongst themselves. The ultimate purpose of these instructions is for Isra'el to act justly and follow ADONAI.

WORD FOCUS

Teitzei: 'To leave or go out.' The way we behave when we 'go out' of our fellowships is important. We take the name of ADONAI with us when we go out, just as we take our family name with us when we leave our homes.

MAIN MESSAGE

This is a message about oppression. ADONAI told Isra'el to remember they were once slaves. They were to treat others the way they wanted to be treated. Some of the instructions were given because of the situations ADONAI knew they would get themselves into, not as commands to be in such situations. ADONAI knows our natural tendencies as sinful people, and makes rules for our own protection.

COMPASSION   JUSTICE   HUMILITY

Promise

Deut 25:19 CJB

"Therefore, when ADONAI your G-d has given you rest from all your surrounding enemies in the land ADONAI your G-d is giving you as your inheritance to possess, you are to blot out all memory of 'Amalek from under heaven. Don't forget!"

Note: Parental discretion advised when reading biblical narrative.

Ki Teitzei Deuteronomy 16:18-21:9 Activity Sheet

Guard Rails

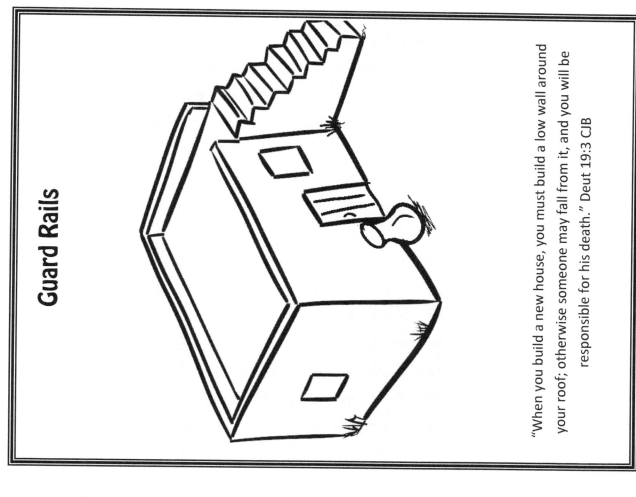

"When you build a new house, you must build a low wall around your roof; otherwise someone may fall from it, and you will be responsible for his death." Deut 19:3 CJB

72 Instructions

Listed are 5 of the 72 instructions given in this Torah portion. Fill in the gaps with the words provided.

home	pretend	plow	men's	seeds

You must not _____ you did not see your brothers cattle, if it strays. You must bring it to your own _____. (Deut 22:1-2)

A woman should not wear _____ clothes. (Deut 22:5)

You are not to sew two kinds of _____ between your rows of vines. (Deut 22:9)

You are not to _____ with an ox and donkey together. (Deut 22:10)

Promise

Isaiah 54:9 CJB

"For me this is like Noach's flood. Just as I swore that no flood like Noach's would ever again cover the earth, so now I swear that never again will I be angry with you or rebuke you."

Yeshayahu

Isaiah 52:13-54:10

STORY SUMMARY

Servant Of ADONAI Foretold: ADONAI, through Yesha'yahu (Isaiah), describes the coming of His servant, who will willingly bear Isra'el's shame despite his innocence. He will become a guilt offering for Isra'el, making many righteous. After this time, he will be given an honoured position and the exiles will return.

WORD FOCUS

Ebed: 'Servant or slave' Yeshua came as the servant of ADONAI. In John 6:38 Yeshua said He had not come to do His own will, but the will of the Father who sent Him.

MAIN MESSAGE

This is the most detailed prophecy in the Torah that speaks of Yeshua. When He came the first time, He fulfilled many of these things. We are eagerly awaiting His return, when we will experience this great favour and covenant of peace.

HOPE   COMFORT   ANTICIPATION

Haffara 49 (Prophets)

Memory Verse

"Therefore I will assign him a share with the great, he will divide the spoil with the mighty, for having exposed himself to death and being counted among the sinners, while actually bearing the sin of many and interceding for the offenders."

Isaiah 52:7 CJB

Did You Know?

Many rabbis often discourage people from reading this part of scripture.

Yeshayahu Isaiah 52:15-54:10 Activity Sheet

Suffering Messiah

"But he was wounded because of our crimes, crushed because of our sins; the disciplining that makes us whole fell on him, and by his bruises* we are healed." Isaiah 53:5 CJB

*or: and in fellowship with him.

Yeshua in Isaiah

Here are just three of the many parallels that can be made with Yeshua and the Isaiah 53 prophecy. Draw a line to match the Newer Testament examples with the quotes from Isaiah 53.

ISAIAH 53

He grew up before him like a tender shoot, and like a root out of dry ground. He had no beauty or majesty to attract us to him, nothing in his appearance that we should desire him.

He was despised and rejected by men, a man of sorrows, and familiar with suffering. Like one from whom men hide their faces, he was despised, and we esteemed him not.

We all, like sheep, have gone astray, each of us has turned to his own way; and the LORD has laid on him the iniquity of us all.

NEWER TESTAMENT

Yeshua was despised, rejected, and suffered. (Mathew 27:21-23)

It would be ADONAI's will that all sin would be laid upon Yeshua! (Gal 1:4)

Yeshua had humble and poor beginnings, not coming as a royal King, but as a commoner. (Luke 2:7)

John 17

B'rit Hadashah 49
(Newer Testament)

STORY SUMMARY

Unity: Yeshua, in prayer to the Father, prays for the unity of His believers; that they will be close to the heart of ADONAI, and will be as one with Him.

WORD FOCUS

Paar: 'Glorify.' This means to reflect ADONAI. We do this by having His Ruach inside us, and living daily with Him.

MEMORY VERSE

"That they may all be one. Just as you, Father, are united with me and I with you, I pray that they may be united with us, so that the world may believe that you sent me." John 17:21 CJB

MAIN MESSAGE

The theme of unity is reflected in the parasha. ADONAI instructed His people to be set apart and unified together. To be truly unified with each other we need to keep our focus on ADONAI, not on each other, so we reflect ADONAI to the world.

PROMISE

"I pray not only for these, but also for those who will trust in me because of their word."
John 17:20 CJB

DID YOU KNOW?

The above verse shows that Yeshua prayed for you especially.

John 17 Activity Sheet

Unity

Unity Object Lesson

Take a toothpick or a twig and snap it. Easy, right? Now take a bundle of tooth picks or sticks and try to break them. It's not so easy now, is it?

This is the same with us. When we try and live life alone, we are easy to break; but if we are united with ADONAI and others of like minded faith, we are harder to break.

Let's learn a Hebrew song about unity.

(Check the internet for the tune.)

Hineh Ma Tov   (English Version)

Hineh ma tov   Behold how good
uma na'im   and how pleasant it is
Shevet achim gam yachad.   For brethren to dwell together

Chorus

Hineh ma tov   In unity
Hineh ma tov   In unity
Lai lai lai lai lai Lai lai lai

Yeshua Prayed

"After Yeshua had said these things, He looked up toward Heaven and said, "Father, the time has come. Glorify your Son, so that the Son may glorify you." John 17:1 CJB

Parasha 50

Memory Verse

"You are agreeing today that *ADONAI* is your G-d and that you will follow His ways; observe His laws, *mitzvot* and rulings; and do what He says."

Deut 26:17 CJB

Did you Know?

Prof. Adam Zertal claims to have found the altar on Mt. Eval, along with sixty pieces of plaster.

בְּרֵאשִׁית Ki Tavo (When you come) Deuteronomy 26:1-29:8(9)*

STORY SUMMARY

Blessings and Curses: ADONAI, through Moshe (Moses), instructs Isra'el about the blessings to be had if they follow ADONAI's ways, and the curses to be had if they do not. Then ADONAI tells them to make an altar on Mt. Eval, the mount of cursing, and write everything they were commanded.

WORD FOCUS

Arar: 'To Curse.' Which is to bring great harm or trouble on someone. This is what would happen to those who came against Isra'el or worshipped other gods.

MAIN MESSAGE

To do right or wrong is often the choice we are faced with. ADONAI is telling us if we do right we will receive blessings and if we do wrong we will receive curses. Have you noticed how some choices lead to good things happening and other choices lead to everything going wrong? Isra'el ended up experiencing the curses because they turned to idols. However, the promise given tells us there will be a time when ADONAI will have a holy people. So there is still hope.

BLESSINGS   CURSES   OBEDIENCE

Promise

Deut 26:18-19 CJB

"In turn *ADONAI* is agreeing today that you are His own unique treasure, as He promised you; that you are to observe all His *mitzvot*, and that He will raise you high above all the nations He has made, in praise, reputation and glory; and that, as He said, you will be a holy people for *ADONAI* your G-d."

Note: Parental discretion advised when reading Biblical narrative

* verse 9 in other translations

Ki Tavo Deuteronomy 26:1-29:8(9) Activity Sheet

Mt. Eval Altar

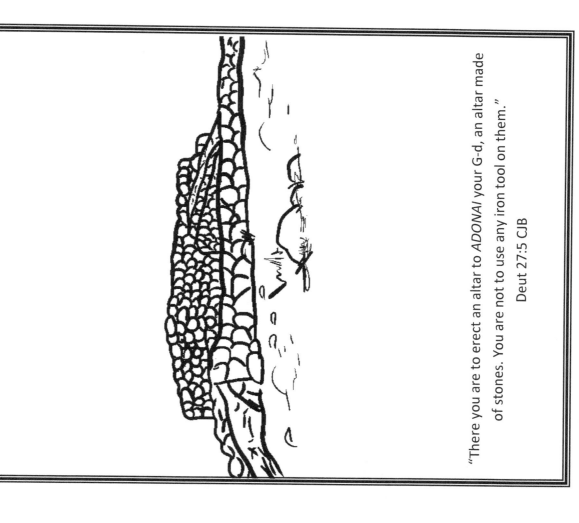

"There you are to erect an altar to *ADONAI* your G-d, an altar made of stones. You are not to use any iron tool on them."

Deut 27:5 CJB

Curses and Blessings

Put a B beside the blessings and a C beside the curses.

Military success

Economic success

Defeat and scorn

Inflammation

Agricultural disaster

Fertility of humans and animals

Abundant food

Madness and blindness

Constantly abused and robbed

Military defeat

Fertility of soil

Yeshayahu

Isaiah 60 1:22

Promise

Isaiah 60:1-2 CJB

"Arise, shine [Yerushalayim], for your light has come, the glory of *ADONAI* has risen over you. For although darkness covers the earth and thick darkness the peoples; on you *ADONAI* will rise; over you will be seen His glory."

STORY SUMMARY

Restoration: Jerusalem is prophesied to be restored and filled with the glory of ADONAI. The exiles will return. The whole world will be drawn to ADONAI's glory, and will acknowledge that ADONAI is G-d. There will be peace and prosperity of ADONAI's people.

WORD FOCUS

Qum, Or: 'Arise, shine.' Stand up and be light. No more oppression. The people will become the light to the nations that they were meant to be.

MAIN MESSAGE

This is the ultimate message of restoration and hope; a promise of ADONAI that is not dependant on our good deeds, but upon His good character. The time of trials is over and the time of rejoicing has come.

HOPE   COMFORT   ANTICIPATION

Haftara 50 (Prophets)

Memory Verse

"...I, *ADONAI*, when the right time comes, will quickly bring it about."

Isaiah 60:22 CJB

Did You Know?

ADONAI will be so bright, the sun and moon will not be needed for light.

Yeshayahu Isaiah 60 Activity Sheet

Coming to the City

"Caravans of camels will cover your land, young camels from Midyan and 'Eifah, all of them coming from Sh'va, bringing gold and frankincense, and proclaiming the praises of ADONAI." Isaiah 60:6 CJB

Transport

Isaiah 60:4-9 list four different ways the people will come. Write these four ways below. The first letters are done for you.

1. N _____ H _____ (verse 4)

2. C _____ (verse 6)

3. F _____ (verse 8)

4. S _____ (verse 9)

Galatians 3:10-14

B'rit Hadashah 50
(Newer Testament)

MAIN MESSAGE

ADONAI knew we would break the Torah, so He made a plan. Because Yeshua took the curse we deserve, we can be saved when we believe in Him. We are to follow ADONAI's commands because we love Him, and want a deeper walk with Him, not because we think it will save us.

PROMISE

"Yeshua the Messiah did this so that in union with Him the Gentiles might receive the blessing announced to Avraham, so that through trusting and being faithful, we might receive what was promised, namely, the Spirit." Galatians 3:14

DID YOU KNOW?

It is impossible to actually keep the Torah without love as the Torah commands us to love ADONAI with our whole heart.

STORY SUMMARY

The Curse of Torah: Paul, through inspiration from ADONAI, explains what the rabbis have missed. Salvation does not come through keeping the rules, but through faith.

WORD FOCUS

Tzaddiq: 'Righteous,' means straight, just, lawful. This does not mean a sinless person, but someone who is walking with ADONAI by faith.

MEMORY VERSE

"For everyone who depends on legalistic observance of *Torah* commands lives under a curse, since it is written, 'Cursed is everyone who does not keep on doing everything written in the Scroll of the *Torah*.'"

Galatians 3:10 CJB

Galatians 3:10-14 Activity Sheet

Trust and Faith

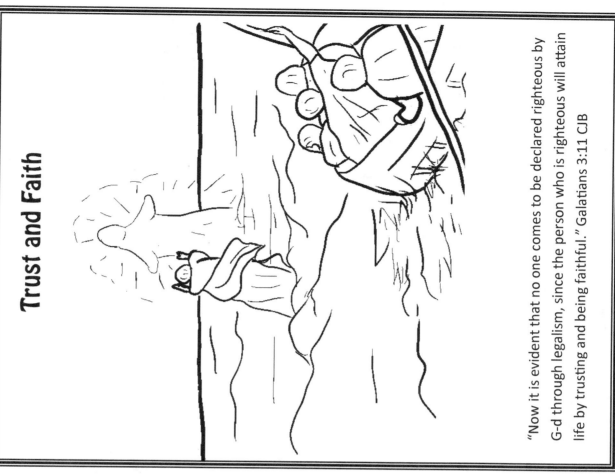

"Now it is evident that no one comes to be declared righteous by G-d through legalism, since the person who is righteous will attain life by trusting and being faithful." Galatians 3:11 CJB

Legalism

It is not keeping the rules that is legalistic, but when we think we can be saved by the good things we do, rather than because of our faith in Yeshua. Put a cross through the legalistic comments and a tick next to the non-legalistic comments.

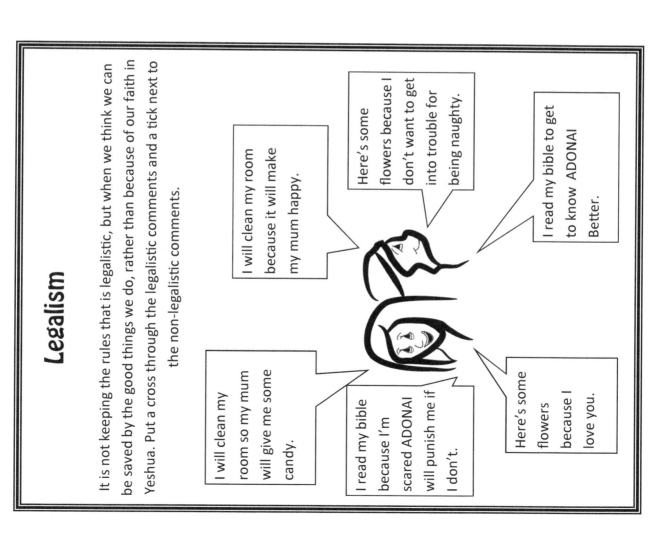

I will clean my room so my mum will give me some candy.

I read my bible because I'm scared ADONAI will punish me if I don't.

Here's some flowers because I love you.

I will clean my room because it will make my mum happy.

Here's some flowers because I don't want to get into trouble for being naughty.

I read my bible to get to know ADONAI Better.

Parasha 51

Nitzavim
פרשת נצבים (Standing) Deuteronomy 29:9(10)*-30:20

Promise
Deut 30:20 CJB

"Loving ADONAI your G-d, paying attention to what He says and clinging to Him — for that is the purpose of your life!..."

Memory Verse

"For this mitzvah which I am giving you today is not too hard for you, it is not beyond your reach."
Deut 30:11 CJB

Did You Know?

Some people who made this covenant were foreigners who joined Isra'el.

STORY SUMMARY

ADONAI Reaffirms The Covenant: Moshe (Moses) finishes his final address to Isra'el by calling for commitment to ADONAI and His ways. This covenant is not only with those who are there, but with all who call themselves Isra'el throughout the generations. Next, the prediction is made that Isra'el will not keep ADONAI's ways, and this will result in exile. Hope is restored by a promise of victory, if they repent and stay close to ADONAI, which He assures is achievable.

WORD FOCUS

Nitzavim: 'You are standing.' This implies firmness and stability. It speaks of the courage and inner strength that comes from an internal knowledge of Torah.

MAIN MESSAGE

Isra'el has matured over the forty years and are now in a position to stand firm. This will also be the case with the final generation before Yeshua returns. They will be witnesses to the entire history of mankind and will be spiritually mature. This happens on a personal level too. The more we grow spiritually, the stronger in faith we become. Then we can stand firm.

OBEDIENCE   STRENGTH   REPENTANCE

* Verse 10 in other translations.

Note: This parasha is to be read as part of a double parasha some years.

Nitzarim Deuteronomy 29:9(10)-30:20 Activity Sheet

The Stand

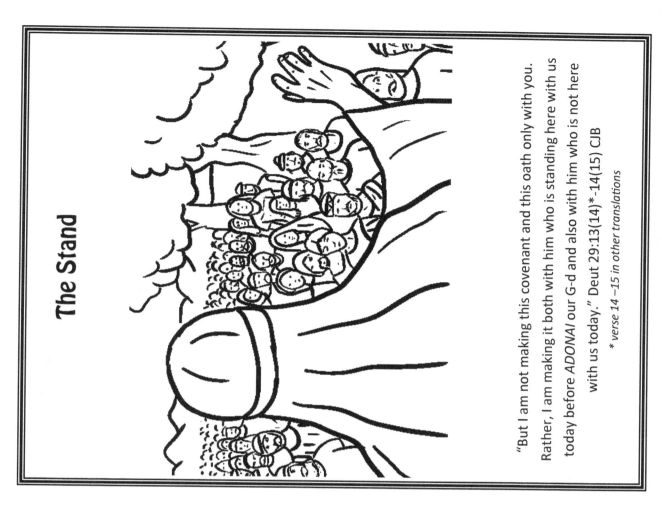

"But I am not making this covenant and this oath only with you. Rather, I am making it both with him who is standing here with us today before ADONAI our G-d and also with him who is not here with us today." Deut 29:13(14)*-14(15) CJB

*verse 14 –15 in other translations

45

Victory

Isaiah 26:3 is one verse that tells us how we will gain victory in our lives. Unscramble the sentence to reveal the answer. The first and last word have been done for you. The Complete Jewish Bible translation has been used here.

perfect whose you he person

trusts rests in desire on preserve

you peace in because

A _____

_____

_____

_____ you.

Yeshayahu

Isaiah 61:10-63:9

STORY SUMMARY

Final Message of Comfort: This Shabbat is the seventh and last Shabbat after Tisha B'Av and the Shiva D'nechemta readings. ADONAI, through Yeshayahu, tells of His desire and plan to 'marry' Isra'el and save her. Believers among the nations are included in this plan.

WORD FOCUS

Shiva D'nechemta: 'Seven weeks of comfort.' This is the time that is just ending when the message of comfort to Isra'el is read in the yearly Torah cycle.

MAIN MESSAGE

ADONAI is ready to cover our sins and mistakes freely because He loves us and wants to save us. We cannot be saved by the good things we do but by accepting this free robe of salvation (Yeshua). Then when we receive His spirit, we will be empowered to live as we should and be part of the great wedding celebration.

Haftara 51 (Prophets)

Memory Verse

"...As a bridegroom rejoices over the bride, your G-d will rejoice over you."

Isaiah 62:5 CJB

Did You Know?

In a wedding, the bride and groom make a covenant with each other. Marriage is an example of the close relationship ADONAI wants with us.

Promise

Isaiah 62:11 CJB

"ADONAI has proclaimed to the end of the earth,

'Say to the daughter of Tziyon,

here, your Salvation is coming!

here, His reward is with Him, and His recompense is before Him.'"

Yeshayahu Isaiah 61:10-63:9 Activity Sheet

Our True Name

Unscramble these words to reveal what Isaiah 62:12 says ADONAI's people will finally be called.

heT

yHlo

oelPpe

Teh

mdRdeeee

fo

INAODA

_____

_____

_____

Bride

"I am so joyful in *ADONAI*! My soul rejoices in my G-d, for He has clothed me in salvation, dressed me with a robe of triumph, like a bridegroom wearing a festive turban, like a bride adorned with her jewels." Isaiah 61:10 CJB

48

Luke 15:11-32

B'rit Hadashah 51
(Newer Testament)

Story Summary

The Prodigal Son: Yeshua tells a parable of a man with two sons. One son wanted to leave home and take his share of his father's money that he would one day inherit. The father agreed, and the son left. He spent all his money and became so poor he had to feed pigs to survive. Finally, the son thought to return home to his father as a servant. However, when his father saw him coming, his father was so full of joy that he honoured the return of his son with a banquet.

WORD FOCUS

Abad: 'Lost' also meaning "to perish or vanish.' The son was lost, but then was found.

MEMORY VERSE

"We had to celebrate and rejoice, because this brother of yours was dead but has come back to life—he was lost but has been found." Luke 15:32 CJB

MAIN MESSAGE

Coming up to Yom Teruah, and Yom Kippur, our heart should be in a state of repentance. When we are truly sorry for our sin, ADONAI will hear from Heaven and make us whole. This can be individually, but it is also for people who claim His name as a group.

PROMISE

"Then, if My people, who bear My name, will humble themselves, pray, seek My face and turn from their evil ways, I will hear from heaven, forgive their sin and heal their land." 2 Chronicles 7:14 CJB

DID YOU KNOW?

Feeding the pigs and eating their food would have been a big insult to a Jew. This showed the son's desperate state.

Luke 15:11-32 Activity Sheet

Prodigal Son

"...But while he was still a long way off, his father saw him and was moved with pity. He ran and threw his arms around him and kissed him warmly." Luke 15:20 CJB

Being Sorry

Return the man back to his home by following the word path to find out what ADONAI thinks of those who return to Him. Rewrite the verse from Luke 15:7 CJB in the right direction. As you come across each letter, write it out in the space provided.

There will be more joy in Heaven over one sinner who turns to G-d

from his sins than over 99 righteous who have no need to repent.

_____

_____

_____

_____

_____

_____

_____

Vayeilech

וַיֵּלֶךְ (He went) Deuteronomy 31:1-30

Parasha 52

Memory Verse

"Therefore, write this song for yourselves and teach it to the people of Isra'el. Have them learn it by heart, so that this song can be a witness for Me against the people of Isra'el."

Deut 31:19 CJB

Did You Know?

Tradition has it that Moshe died on his birthday.

STORY SUMMARY

ADONAI Prepares Moshe for his Death: Moshe (Moses) is now 120 years old. It is nearly his time to be put to rest. Moshe passes the leadership to Y'hoshua, and writes down the Torah according to ADONAI's instructions. Moshe gives this Torah to the Levites to keep next to the Ark of the Covenant. It is to be read during the festival of Sukkot, every seventh year, so they will never forget. Then, ADONAI tells Moshe that the people will turn away from Him. He instructed Moshe to write a song and teach it to the congregation.

WORD FOCUS

Avar: 'Crossing over.' This is the root word of 'Hebrew.' To become a Hebrew means to 'cross over.'

MAIN MESSAGE

The four witnesses of ADONAI are, the written instructions, the song of Moshe, the heavens and the earth. They are to remind Isra'el of their disobedience and cause them to seek repentance. Just as Moshe would not be the one to lead Isra'el to the Promised Land, salvation does not come by Moshe, nor the law of Moshe, but by the saving blood and grace of Yeshua. He is the only way we can cross over from death to life.

OBEDIENCE   REPENTANCE   SALVATION

Promise

Deut 31:7 CJB

"Next Moshe summoned Y'hoshua, and in the sight of all Isra'el, said to him, 'Be strong, be bold, for you are going with this people into the land ADONAI swore to their ancestors He would give them. You will be the one causing them to inherit it.'"

Vaeilech Deuteronomy 31:1-30 Activity Sheet

The Torah

Can you remember five instructions that Moshe would have written down.

1. _____

_____

2. _____

_____

3. _____

_____

4. _____

_____

5. _____

_____

Reading the Torah

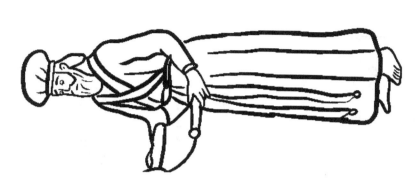

"Moshe gave them these orders: 'At the end of every seven years, during the festival of *Sukkot* in the year of *sh'mittah*, when all Isra'el have come to appear in the presence of *ADONAI* at the place He will choose, you are to read this *Torah* before all Isra'el, so that they can hear it.'" Deut 31:10-11 CJB

Yeshayahu

Isaiah 55:6-56:8

Promise

Isaiah 55:11 CJB

"So is my word that goes out from my mouth — it will not return to me unfulfilled; but it will accomplish what I intend, and cause to succeed what I sent it to do."

STORY SUMMARY

A Great Hope: ADONAI does not leave His message at the fact that His people will turn away from Him. He continues through His prophets to bring the message of hope, if they turn around. Here again ADONAI is calling His children to return and showing them a glimpse of what it will be like if they do. They will live in peace and happiness. Creation will be glad, and the land will be blessed. ADONAI also says He cares about people keeping the Shabbat.

WORD FOCUS

Darash: 'Seek.' Other words to describe darash are to 'ask, question or enquire.' ADONAI wants us to come to Him with our questions and to talk to Him.

MAIN MESSAGE

This message of hope is also to be sung. Earlier on in Yeshayahu, ADONAI tells His people to sing out. We are never left without hope. Who this group will include at the final gathering depends on who will turn around. Although it is a message to the whole of Isra'el, it is individuals who make up Isra'el. Let's choose to be counted in that number by staying close to ADONAI, and by keeping His Shabbat.

ENCOURAGEMENT   HOPE   PROMISE

Haftara 52 (Prophets)

Memory Verse

"Happy is the person who does this, anyone who grasps it firmly, who keeps *Shabbat* and does not profane it, and keeps himself from doing any evil."

Isaiah 56:2 CJB

Did You Know?

Yeshua is the 'word' that was sent out from the mouth of ADONAI in the form of a man.

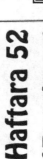

Yeshayahu Isaiah 55:6-56:8 Activity Sheet

Seek ADONAI

"Seek *ADONAI* while He is available, call on Him while He is still nearby. Let the wicked person abandon his way and the evil person his thoughts; let him return to *ADONAI*, and He will have mercy on him; let him return to our G-d, for He will freely forgive."

Isaiah 55:6-7 CJB

Following ADONAI

The Shabbat is on the seventh day of the week, Saturday. Circle every seventh letter to reveal the missing word. What else did ADONAI say was important to do in Isaiah 56:1.

S	V	K	R	F	L	(J)	G
A	O	Q	B	Z	U	F	X
H	F	W	E	S	M	C	P
T	Y	D	T	V	N	L	O
R	D	I	J	E	Z	Q	S
X	C	A	U	F	M	K	C
E	R	S	P				

Observe _ _ _ _ _ _ _, do what is right.

Hebrews 13:5-8

B'rit Hadashah 52
(Newer Testament)

STORY SUMMARY

Live Well: Shaul (Paul) warns the new believers to not get trapped by a love a money, but trust in the provisions of ADONAI. He encouraged them to live their lives with the same trust the great leaders of the past had. He reminds them that Yeshua has not changed but is the same as always.

WORD FOCUS

Azad: "Leave, forsake, lose.' ADONAI will not lose us. He knows where we are at all times.

MEMORY VERSE

" Therefore, we say with confidence, 'ADONAI is my helper; I will not be afraid — what can a human being do to me?'"

MAIN MESSAGE

This passage quotes the Torah portion this week in verse 5. The same was true for the believers in Shaul's day as it was for Isra'el when ADONAI first said it. It is still true today. ADONAI will never fail you or abandon you.

PROMISE

"Yeshua the Messiah is the same yesterday, today and forever." Hebrews 13:8 CJB

DID YOU KNOW?

Hebrews is written to the Jewish believers.

Luke 15:11-32 Activity Sheet

Love of Money

The reason ADONAI is against the love of money is that it can take the place of Him. We can easily fall into relying on our money instead on relying on ADONAI to provide for our needs.

List the things you love that have been brought with money. Ask yourself if each of these things is more important than ADONAI in your life.

Love of Money

"Keep your lives free from the love of money; and be satisfied with what you have; for G-d himself has said, 'I will never fail you or abandon you.'" Hebrews 13:5 CJB

Parasha 53   הַאֲזִינוּ   Ha'Azinu

(Hear) Deuteronomy 32:1-52

Memory Verse

"Hear, oh heavens, as I speak!

Listen, earth, to the words from my mouth!"

Deut 32:1 CJB

Did You Know?

Revelation fifteen talks about the song of Moshe being sung at the end of time.

STORY SUMMARY

Song of Moshe: ADONAI, commands Moshe to write a song and teach it to Isra'el as a witness. They are to memorise it, so they will never forget the message. This is not a song only for that generation but for the future. ADONAI is defending His right to bring judgement upon a world who has turned away from Him, despite His tender leading. They have persecuted His servants and corrupted the land, but He will come and set things right.

WORD FOCUS

Elyon: 'Most High G-d.' This is a title used in verse eight of this song.

MAIN MESSAGE

Although this is a song of judgement, there is hope for the righteous. Their suffering will not go unnoticed, and justice will be served. By remembering the song of Moshe, we remind ourselves in tough times, and dark times to keep holding on because victory is on the way.

HOPE   JUSTICE   JUDGEMENT

Promise

Deut 31:21 CJB

"Then, after many calamities and troubles have come upon them, this song will testify before them as a witness, because their descendants will still be reciting it and will not have forgotten it. For I know how they think even now, even before I have brought them into the land about which I swore."

Ha Azinu Deuteronomy 32:1-52 Activity Sheet

Song of Moshe

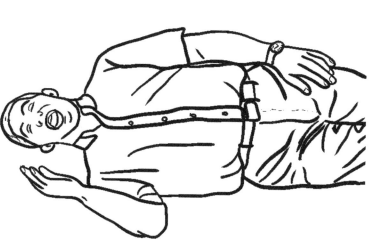

"Sing out, you nations, about His people! For He will avenge the blood of His servants. He will render vengeance to His adversaries and make atonement for the land of His people."

Deut 32:43 CJB

Songs

Many songs have words that rhyme. Can you think of rhyming words for these words? Maybe you could use them in a song.

Bless _____

True _____

Great _____

Praise _____

Just _____

Shine _____

Sh'mu'el Bet

2 Samuel 53 *

Promise

2 Samuel 22:26-28 CJB

"With the merciful, you are merciful; with the champion of purity, you are pure; with the honest, you are honest; but with the crooked you are cunning. People afflicted, you save; but when your eyes are on the haughty, you humble them."

STORY SUMMARY

David's Song: David sings praise to ADONAI for saving him from his enemy, King Saul. He is confident in his righteousness and standing with ADONAI.

WORD FOCUS

Sheol: 'The grave, pit, abode of the dead.' This is what David was saved from.

MAIN MESSAGE

In contrast to Moshe's song about judgement, David's song is about being saved from death, and given life. David's confidence can inspire us to have confidence that we too are saved if we walk with ADONAI, and He will count us as blameless in His sight. We do not need to fear the judgement.

* Also see Shabbat Shuva in Special Shabbat section for Yom Teruah lesson.

Haftara 53 (Prophets)

Memory Verse

"ADONAI is my Rock, my fortress and deliverer, the G-d who is my Rock, in whom I find shelter, my shield, the power that saves me, my stronghold and my refuge. My saviour, you have saved me from violence."

2 Samuel 22:3 CJB

Did you Know?

David made mistakes, but he was faithful to ADONAI.

2 Samuel 22:1-55 Activity Sheet

Faithfulness

"For I have kept the ways of ADONAI, I have not done evil by leaving my G-d; for all his rulings were before me, I did not depart from his regulations. I was pure-hearted toward Him and kept myself from my sin."

2 Samuel 22:22-24 CJB

Rescue

ADONAI rescued David. Rescue the personal qualities David believed made him worthy, by circling them. You can find them in 2 Samuel 22: 21-28 CJB

stubborn

Kept ADONAI'S rulings before me

uprightness

Idol worshiper

Did not do evil

Murderous

Pure Hearted

Honest

Doubter

Clean hands

Selfish

Kept the ways of ADONAI

Didn't depart from ADONAI's regulations

Acts
2:1-47

B'rit Hadashah 53
(Newer Testament)

STORY SUMMARY

The Ruach Hakodesh: The talmidim (apostles) receive the promised Ruach Hakodesh, and are empowered to preach the good news and immerse. They also have a strong sense of unity. Because of these things, they add to their number each day.

WORD FOCUS

Yoreh: Early Rain   **Malkosh:** Later Rain

Matar: Rain   **Geshem:** Heavy Rain

MEMORY VERSE

"All Scripture is G-d-breathed and is valuable for teaching the truth, convicting of sin, correcting faults and training in right living." 2 Timothy 3:16

MAIN MESSAGE

The Ruach Hakodesh was 'poured out' like rain. The song of Moshe likens the words of ADONAI to rain. Both ADONAI's Word and His Spirit are linked together, that is why both of them are symbolized by water and rain. They are both needed in our life in order for us to grow spiritually and be a true community of believers, who are ready for the Messiah's return.

PROMISE

"After this, I will pour out my Spirit on all humanity. Your sons and daughters will prophesy, your old men will dream dreams, your young men will see visions."

Joel 3:1 (2:28)* CJB

DID YOU KNOW?

Rain is crucial for life. Without rain, the land dries up, and the people die.

* verse in other translations

Acts 2:1-47 Activity Sheet

Ruach Filled Believers

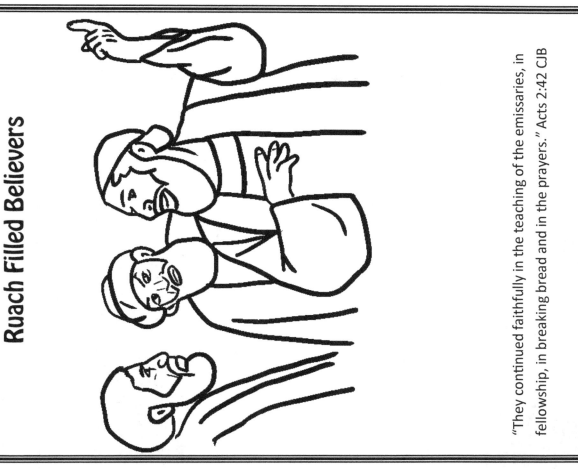

"They continued faithfully in the teaching of the emissaries, in fellowship, in breaking bread and in the prayers." Acts 2:42 CJB

Rain

Catch the rain drops in order to reveal what ADONAI said in Deuteronomy 32:2 CJB.

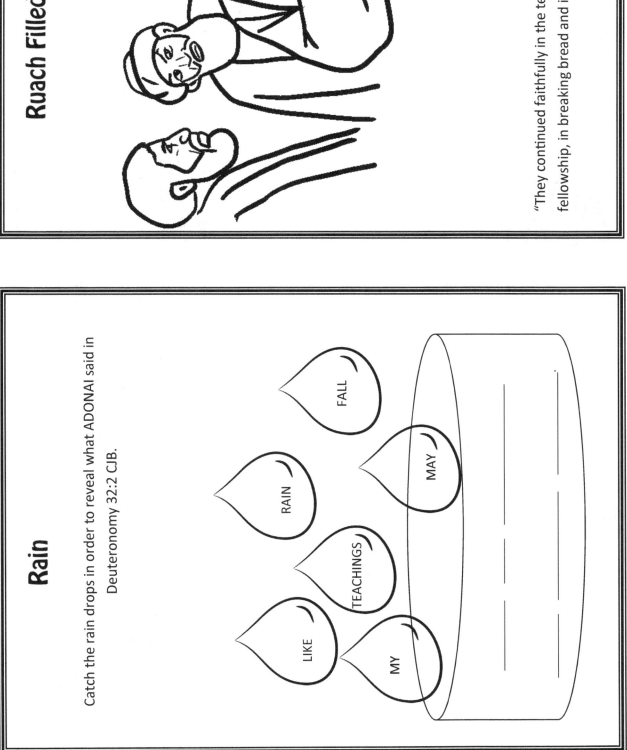

FALL

RAIN

MAY

TEACHINGS

LIKE

MY

Parasha 54

Vezot Haberakah

פרשת וזאת הברכה

(This is the blessing)
Deuteronomy 33:1-34:12

Memory Verse

"He truly loves the peoples — all His holy ones are in your hand; sitting at your feet, they receive your instruction."

Deut 33:3 CJB

Did You Know?

Nobody has found the grave of Moshe. Jude 1:9 mentions the angel Mikha'el arguing over his body.

STORY SUMMARY

Moshe Blesses the Tribes: Moshe, in his final words to Isra'el, pronounces a blessing over each tribe. A different blessing is given according to their strengths and purposes.

Moshe Dies: After the blessing, ADONAI takes Moshe to Mt. N'vo to show him the land. There he dies and is buried.

WORD FOCUS

The first letter of the Torah is 'bet (ב)', meaning 'house'. The last word in the Torah is 'Isra'el', who are the children chosen to live in the house. The first and last letters of the Torah are 'bet' and 'lamed (ל)' which spell 'Lev'; this means 'heart'. The Torah reveals the heart of the Father to those living in His house.

MAIN MESSAGE

ADONAI views us as children, all unique with different skill, abilities and interests. Therefore, He gives us callings in life that are in line with those gifts and talents. He can also give us gifts and talents according to our calling. This again shows how ADONAI knows us all individually. Although Moshe was 120, he did not die from old age. Chapter 34:7 says his eyes were not dim, nor his body failing. Just as Moshe had to die before Isra'el could enter the land, so too Yeshua had to die before we can enter the promised Land.

BLESSING   FAMILY   RELATIONSHIP

Promise

Deut 33:3 CJB

"Then a king arose in Yeshurun when the leaders of the people were gathered, all the tribes of Isra'el together."

Vezot Haberakah Deuteronomy 33:1-34:12 Activity Sheet

Moshe's Farewell

"This is the blessing that Moshe, the man of G-d, spoke over the people of Isra'el before his death."

Deut 33:1 CJB

Blessings

Follow the lines to find the unique blessings given to each tribe.

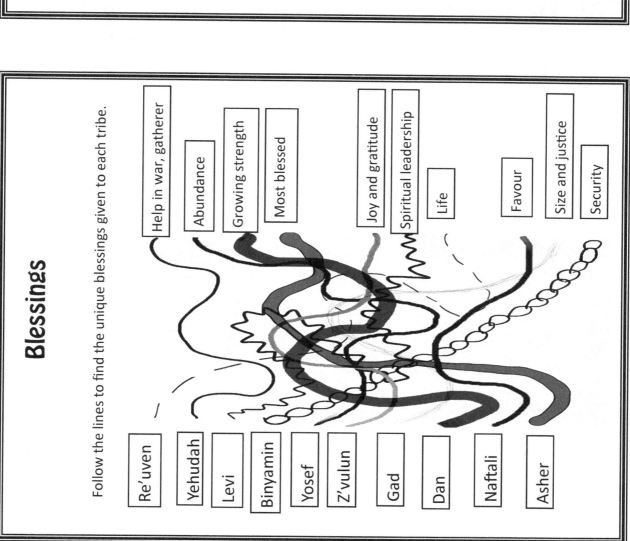

Re'uven

Yehudah

Levi

Binyamin

Yosef

Z'vulun

Gad

Dan

Naftali

Asher

Help in war, gatherer

Abundance

Growing strength

Most blessed

Joy and gratitude

Spiritual leadership

Life

Favour

Size and justice

Security

Y'hoshua

Joshua 1:1-18

Promise

Joshua 1:5 CJB

"No one will be able to withstand you as long as you live. Just as I was with Moshe, so I will be with you. I will neither fail you nor abandon you."

STORY SUMMARY

Y'hoshua is Encouraged: Y'hoshua has just become the leader of Isra'el since Moshe has died. He has the huge task ahead of him of taking the land. This will require courage, boldness, and strength, all of which ADONAI pronounces over Y'hoshua before hand.

WORD FOCUS

Chazak: 'To be or grow strong—strengthen.' ADONAI did not expect Y'hoshua to grow strong in his own might, but by staying close to ADONAI.

MAIN MESSAGE

How do you feel when someone gives you words of encouragement? Does it help you believe in yourself? The words that we speak over people are very powerful. We should use our words to love people, not hurt them. ADONAI spoke words of life over Y'hoshua as a blessing for the task set before him. ADONAI does not want us to run away and hide in the face of trials, but to face them with courage, and be strengthened through them, by trusting in Him.

LIFE   ENCOURAGEMENT   COURAGE

Haftara 54 (Prophets)

Memory Verse

"Haven't I ordered you, 'Be strong, be bold'? So don't be afraid or downhearted, because ADONAI/your G-d is with you wherever you go."

Joshua 1:9 CJB

Did You Know?

The giants Isra'el defeated were at least three times their size. With ADONAI anything is possible.

Joshua 1:1-18 Activity Sheet

Crossing Over

To inherit the land, Isra'el had to cross over the Jordan. When we accept Yeshua, we cross over from death to life. Cross this river by choosing the life words not the death words.

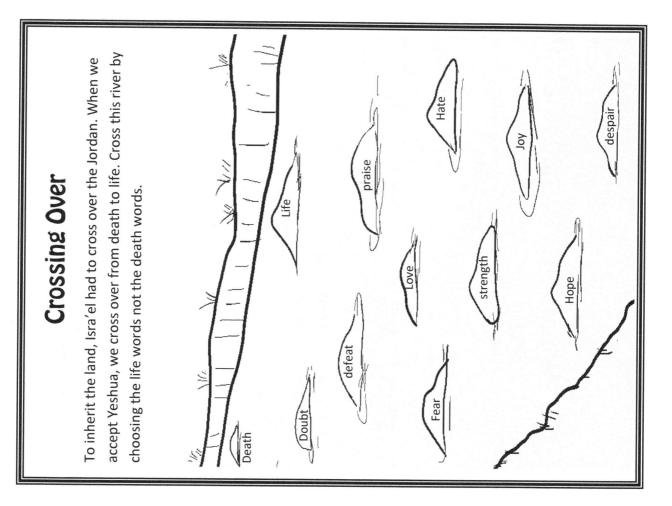

The Great Leader Y'hoshua

"Be strong, be bold; for you will cause this people to inherit the land I swore to their fathers I would give them."

Joshua 1:6 CJB

Hebrews 8 and 9

B'rit Hadashah 54
(Newer Testament)

STORY SUMMARY

Yeshua Our High Priest: Shaul explains how the pattern of the Tabernacle in the wilderness is a copy of the one in Heaven. Yeshua is now our High Priest who, once only, takes His own blood into the most holy place as a perfect sacrifice for our unintentional sin. This purifies our conscience as well as our physical body, and brings restoration.

WORD FOCUS

Yamin: 'Right Hand.' In this case, being at the right hand of the Father, symbolises equal position.

MEMORY VERSE

"For the Messiah has entered a Holiest Place which is not man-made and merely a copy of the true one, but into Heaven itself, in order to appear now on our behalf in the very presence of G-d." Romans 9:24 CJB

MAIN MESSAGE

At Yom Kippur we are called to fast and repent. There is no sacrifice for sinning on purpose, but there is forgiveness if we confess our sin. If we accept Yeshua's blood sacrifice for us and let His Ruach Ha Kodesh work in our life, He promises to cleanse us and make us new. His sacrifice only needed to happen once. However, because sin is still in the world, our repentance needs to happen more often. This day helps us remember to repent.

PROMISE

"For G-d so loved the world that He gave His only and unique Son, so that everyone who trusts in Him may have eternal life, instead of being utterly destroyed." John 3:16 CJB

DID YOU KNOW?

Instead of fasting, some children under twelve or thirteen fast from things such as technology or sugar. If you are too young to fast, what could you give up for a day?

Hebrews 8-9 Activity Sheet

5 Steps of Repentance

These are the 5 Steps of Repentance. When you think you know them, make a skit or write a story to show you understand. If you have trouble with any of these steps, pray and ask ADONAI to help you.

1. **Know** what you did was wrong.

2. **Feel sorry** for what you have done.

3. **Confess.** Tell the person what you did and say you are sorry. If this is not possible, confess to ADONAI and maybe a parent.

4. **Forsake** the sin. Try your best not to do that again and ask ADONAI to help with this.

5. Make **Restitution.** If possible, make it up to the person by doing something for him/her that shows you are truly sorry.

And always remember to have a **forgiving** attitude when someone has wronged you.

Second Coming

"So also the Messiah, having been offered once to bear the sins of many, will appear a second time, not to deal with sin, but to deliver those who are eagerly waiting for Him."

Hebrews 9:28 CJB

Promise

Hosea 14:5(4)* CJB

"I will heal

their

disloyalty,

I will love

them

freely;

for my

anger has

turned

from him."

* verse 4 in other translations.

Haftara 53A (Prophets)

Shabbat Shuva

Hosea 14:2-10, Micah 7:18-20, Joel 2:15-27

Memory Verse

"Blow the *shofar* in Tziyon! Proclaim a holy fast, call for a solemn assembly."

Joel 2:15 CJB

Did You Know?

Revelation 8:11 talks about the shofar being blown before the return of Yeshua.

STORY SUMMARY

Forgiveness: In these three passages, ADONAI says He will stop being angry for the rebellion of His children. He will hear their repentant cries and restore them. The shofar is blown as a call to war. ADONAI will intervene for His children, who are under attack.

WORD FOCUS

Shabbat Shuva: 'The Sabbath of Return.' This is a season of repentance. When we are sorry, the next step is to turn around and come back to the truth we know.

MAIN MESSAGE

Yom Teruah (Feast of Trumpets) is the day in Leviticus 23:24 when Isra'el was commanded to have a shabbat and blow the shofar. This is in preparation for Yom Kippur. During this time, we should be praying that ADONAI will show us if, and how, we have wronged Him and to give us a true spirit of repentance.

HOPE   COMFORT   ANTICIPATION

Shabbat Shuva Activity Sheet

Yom Teruah

Complete the wordsearch with these words from Leviticus 23:24

```
R Z L L T G E H M J R C Y A D
E P E S L L I O H P O R N Y F
M N Z H P E N R X N A H V P Y
E T T O K T T B V B Y Y K O G
M B E F H T E O W I T H U T L
B P F A D Y C T I M X G T D H
E I O R W A M P E T S R I F T
R G R H T P C H B L Y X Y V N
I L B I S R A E L L P P Q T E
N E O J I A O V J A A M T Z V
G N D E C N U O N N A S O B E
S T J D Y N N T Y I V X T C S
R E S L T E B L H R P H S S U
G N U G X U O R W E Q C E T C
S U V L D H M J J C R V R E E
```

ANNOUNCED
BLASTS
COMPLETE
CONVOCATION
DAY
FIRST
FOR
HOLY
ISRAEL
MONTH

PEOPLE
REMEMBERING
REST
SEVENTH
SHOFAR
TELL
THE
WITH
YOU

Blowing the Shofar

"Tell the people of Isra'el, 'In the seventh month, the first of the month is to be for you a day of complete rest for remembering, a holy convocation announced with blasts on the *shofar*."

Leviticus 23:24 CJB

SUKKOT

What is Sukkot?

Sukkot is the Feast of Tabernacles, where Isra'el is commanded to live in sukkah's/ booths or temporary dwellings for 7-8 days. It is the seventh and final feast for the year, and is considered to be the most important. It is a time of joy and thanksgiving. The sukkah is to remind Isra'el of the temporary dwellings in the wilderness after coming out of Egypt. It is also a reminder of our ultimate dwelling place with ADONAI in the future.

When is Sukkot?

Sukkot starts on the 15th day of the 7th month in the Hebrew calendar.

Where does the Bible talk about Sukkot?

Sukkot is mentioned in a number of places, but the places it is commanded are: Leviticus 23:34-36, 40 and Deuteronomy 16:13-17

Why is it important today?

Many believe Yeshua came as a baby to 'dwell' among us during the festival of Sukkot. ADONAI's appointed times are His special appointments with His children. They also show us His great plan of salvation. If there's any appointment you don't want to miss, it is an appointment with ADONAI.

A Sukkot Activity:

Construct a sukkah out of iceblock sticks and either hot glue or string.

Decorate it with plastic greenery on the top. Draw, colour and cut out different fruit to stick on also. You could use this as a table centre piece during the festival.

Haftara 48

3 and all the ends of the earth will see

2 In the sight of every nation

4 the salvation of our G-d

1 ADONAI Has bared His holy arm

B'rit Hadashah 48 N/A

Parasha 48

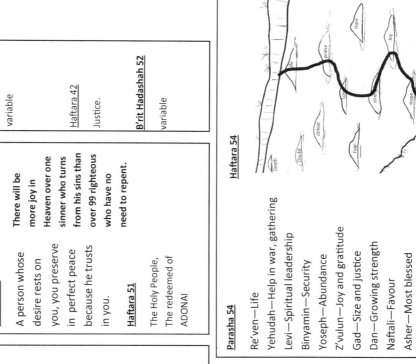

- Enchanter — A person who has/claims to have magical powers.
- Necromancer — A person who uses magic to talk to the dead
- Soothsayer — A person who uses special powers and ceremonies to predict future events
- Diviner — A person who sees future events through dreams or visions
- Sorcerer/Wizard — A person who uses magic or spells

Parasha 47
Variable

B'rit Hadashah 47

Yes indeed I tell you that until Heaven and earth pass away, not so much as a yud or a stroke will pass from the Torah— not until everything that must happen has happened.

Parasha 46
Variable but may include idols or items used in witchcraft

Haftara 46
"As surely as I am alive, you will wear them all like jewels, adorn yourself with them like a bride."

B'rit Hadashah 46
Answers may vary but some good words are: Content, Meek, Humble, Polite, Unselfish/selfless, Patient

Parasha 45
Variable

Haftara 45
Ya'kov and or Isra'el

B'rit Hadasha 45
N/A

B'rit Hadashah 44
1:A, 2:B, 3:B, 4:A

Haftara 44

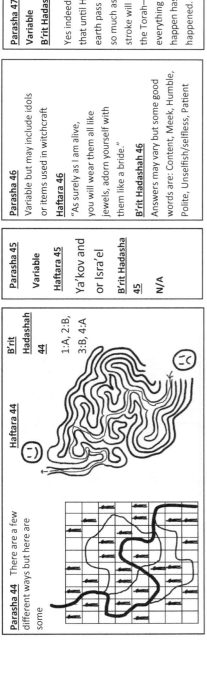

Parasha 44
There are a few different ways but here are some

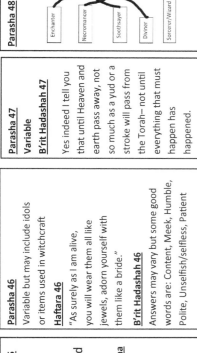

Parasha 52
variable

Haftara 42
Justice.

B'rit Hadashah 52
variable

B'rit Hadashah 51
There will be more joy in Heaven over one sinner who turns from his sins than over 99 righteous who have no need to repent.

Parasha 51
A person whose desire rests on you, you preserve in perfect peace because he trusts in you.

Haftara 51
The Holy People, The redeemed of ADONAI

Parasha 49
Pretend, home, men's, seed, plow

Haftara 49
ISAIAH 53 — NEWER TESTAMENT

He grew up before him like a tender shoot, and like a root out of dry ground; He had no beauty or majesty to attract us to him, nothing in his appearance that we should desire him.

Yeshua was despised, rejected, and suffered Matthew 27:21(23)

He was despised and rejected by men, a man of sorrows, and familiar with suffering. Like one from whom men hide their faces, he was despised, and we esteemed him not.

It would be ADONAI's will that all sin would be laid upon Yeshua (Gal 1:4)

We all, like sheep, have gone astray, each of us has turned to his own way; and the LORD has laid on him the iniquity of us all.

Yeshua had humble and poor beginnings, not coming as a royal King, but as a commoner. (Luke 2:7)

Haftara 40
Nurses Hips, Camels, Flying, Ships.

Parasha 50

- Agricultural disaster — C
- Economic success — B
- Fertility of humans and animals — B
- Defeat and scorn — C
- Abundant food — B
- Inflammation — C
- Military defeat — B
- Madness and blindness — C
- Fertility of soil — B
- Constantly abused and robbed — C
- Military success — C

B'rit Hadashah 50

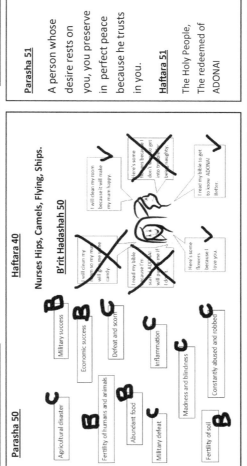

I will clean my room because it will make my mum happy.

Here's some flowers because I don't get into trouble by being naughty.

I will clean my room so my mum will give me candy.

I read my bible to get to know ADONAI Better.

I read my bible because I'm scared ADONAI will punish me if I don't.

Here's some flowers because I love you.

Parasha 54
- Re'ven—Life
- Yehudah—Help in war, gathering
- Levi—Spiritual leadership
- Binyamin—Security
- Yoseph—Abundance
- Z'vulun—Joy and gratitude
- Gad—Size and justice
- Dan—Growing strength
- Naftali—Favour
- Asher—Most blessed

Haftara 54

B'rit Hadasha 53
May my teachings fall like rain

Kept ADONAI's rulings before me
uprightness
Idol worshiper
stubborn
Did not do evil
Murderous
Honest
Clean hands
Selfish
Doubter
Pure Hearted
Kept the ways of ADONAI
Didn't depart from ADONAI's regulations

Haftara 53 B

Haftara 53 A

```
R + + L + + E + + E + M + + C Y A D
E + + S L L + O + + O + + + + Y
M + + H P E N + + N + + + + + + O +
E + + O + T T + V + + + + + O + +
M + E F H + E O W I T H U + +
B P F A + + C T + + + + + + + H
E + + O R + A + + E T S R I F T
R + + R + T + + + B L L + + + + N
I + + + I S R A E L L P + + + E
N + O + + + + + + A M + + V
G N D E C N U O N N A S O + E
+ + + + + + + + + L Y + + + T C S
+ + + + + + + + L H + + + + + S S +
+ + + + + + + + + O + + E + +
+ + + + + + + H + + + + + R + +
```

Parasha 53
Answers will vary but may include:
- mess, less
- blue, shoe, glue,
- who, you wait,
- late, hate, gate,
- mate graze, haze,
- phase, raise,
- must, rust, dust,
- crust, trust
- wine, pine, dine,
- line, mine

References and Websites Used

In order of Appearance

Bible.org

biblehub.com

messianic-torah-truth-seeker.org

bible.ca

Hebcal.Betemunah.org

Bibleprophecytruth.com

Richard Elofer

Wikimedia.org

reformjudaism.org

myjewishlearning.com

hebrew4christians.com

Theworkofgodschildren.org

coolnotions.com

flickr.com

edensbridge.org

answers.yahoo.com

merriam-webster.com

yourlivingwaters.com

Israelnationalnews.com

shechem.org

wikipedia.org

wikihow.com

wildbranch.org

ucg.org

mindfultorah.com

clal.org

Torah.org

jhom.com

morguefiles

clipart.com

adventistreport.com

CPSIA information can be obtained
at www.ICGtesting.com
Printed in the USA
BVHW01s1016060918
526665BV00004B/19/P